contents

THE HOLOCAUST IN HISTORY	1
LEARNING ABOUT THE HOLOCAUST	3
THE JEWISH TRADITION	5
ANTISEMITISM	7
THE RISE OF HITLER	9
THE 'FINAL SOLUTION'	21
THE CAMP SYSTEM	23
RESISTANCE	25
A SPECTRUM OF VICTIMS	27
DEATH MARCHES	29

The Holocaust in History

'The story of the Holocaust can never be told fully... My greatest desire is to see future generations learn about and learn from our experiences'.

Kitty Hart-Moxon, liberated at Salzwedel, 14 April, 1945.

When we look back at history, we often find that both progress and tragedy stand out. Progress stands out because we like to see how developments in culture, society, the arts and science have added to the richness of human experience. Tragedy, on the other hand, stands out because we feel the need to understand the sufferings of our fellow human beings. The Twentieth Century brought its share of both progress and tragedy as never before. The world moved on, using the powers of science and technology. Sadly, this progress was also put to terrible use, as more people were killed in wars and genocide than in any previous generation.

Over 150 million innocent people have been murdered in the last hundred years because of who they happened to be, many with weapons more cleverly made than ever before. Mass murder and genocide have become more and more frequent and the chances of innocent lives being wasted have increased. Armenians, Jews, Gypsies, Cambodians, Rwandan Tutsis and Bosnian Muslims - to name but a few - have experienced genocide in the Twentieth Century.

Among the many tragedies of mass killing, the Nazi regime of Adolf Hitler gives particular cause for concern. In the heartland of 'civilised' Europe, the Nazis created a racial state, where terror and persecution became the norm. There were many victims of Nazi policy. Any group or individual who did not fit into the Nazi ideal was persecuted. The Jews, however, became a specific target of Hitler's racial state. The result was the most devastating and organised policy of mass murder, in which millions of people died, not because of what they believed in, nor what they did, nor what they said, but simply because they were Jews.

Learning about history is not just about trying to memorise dates and facts, but about trying to understand the experiences of other people in the past. To piece together a more complete picture, we have to collect evidence from a number of different sources.

It is not always easy to see at first sight how interesting these sources can be. Often they just look like old bits of yellow paper, with foreign languages scrawled across them. But a closer look can reveal a lot about historical events, about places, and most importantly about people.

When we are learning about the Holocaust, we depend on a wide range of sources to help us understand what happened. The Nazis tried to cover their actions, so we first have to find the clues; then we have to try and make sense of them. Try to remember, though, that these sources are not just interesting; they are also about a tragic period in history, and about how that history affected people and their lives.

"write and record."
These were reported to be the final words of 81 year old historian Simon Dubnow when he was shot by the Nazis in Riga in December 1941.

Learning about the Holocaust

finding and using evidence

These are some of the sources you might find here, or in other books and museums.

Eyewitness accounts: These include diaries and letters, escapees' reports and the writing of victims trying to inform history. Nazis wrote reports and letters. People who looked on also reported what they saw.

Documents: There are many German documents, including speech transcripts, newspapers, and reports sent back to Berlin.

Photographs, film and artefacts: Photographs and film are very important for visualising what happened. The problem is that most photos were taken, and most films were made, by the Nazis for propaganda, so we have to be careful how we use them. Artefacts help us to understand that these events really happened.

Trials: There are court transcripts and media reports of war crimes trials such as those in Nuremberg or Jerusalem.

Survivor Testimony: There are still many people alive today who were victims of the Nazis. Their books, tapes and video testimonies are very important to help us understand the personal meaning of the Holocaust.

'The testimony of those who survived constitutes the main record of what was done to the Jews during those years. The murderers also kept records, often copious ones. But the victims, the six million who were done to death, could leave no record'. *Sir Martin Gilbert, British historian.*

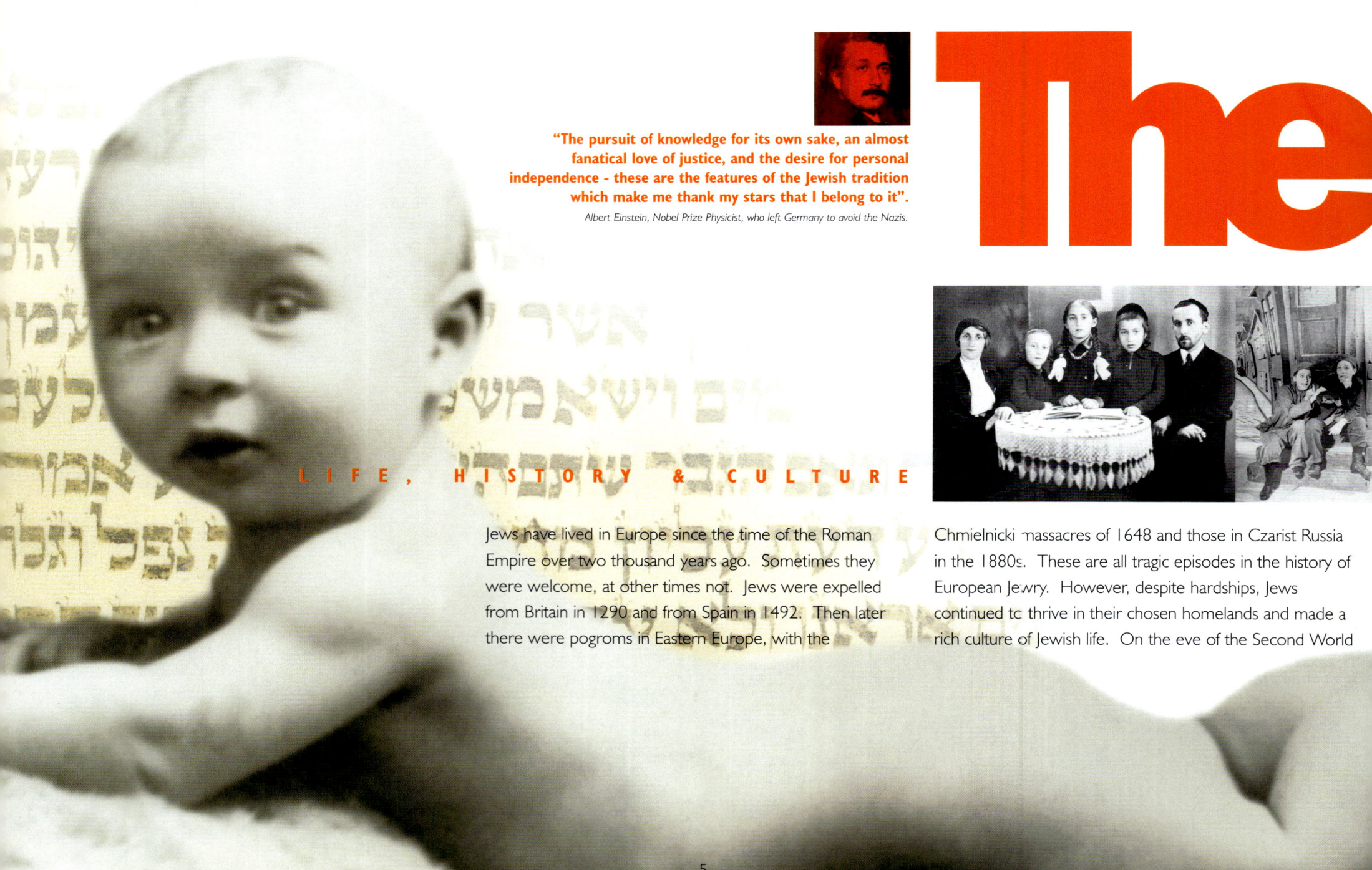

"The pursuit of knowledge for its own sake, an almost fanatical love of justice, and the desire for personal independence - these are the features of the Jewish tradition which make me thank my stars that I belong to it".

Albert Einstein, Nobel Prize Physicist, who left Germany to avoid the Nazis.

The

LIFE, HISTORY & CULTURE

Jews have lived in Europe since the time of the Roman Empire over two thousand years ago. Sometimes they were welcome, at other times not. Jews were expelled from Britain in 1290 and from Spain in 1492. Then later there were pogroms in Eastern Europe, with the Chmielnicki massacres of 1648 and those in Czarist Russia in the 1880s. These are all tragic episodes in the history of European Jewry. However, despite hardships, Jews continued to thrive in their chosen homelands and made a rich culture of Jewish life. On the eve of the Second World

Jewish tradition

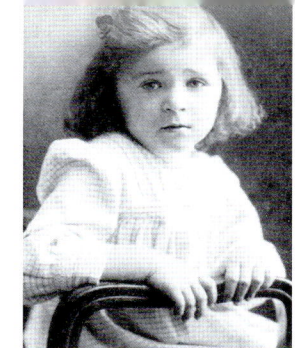

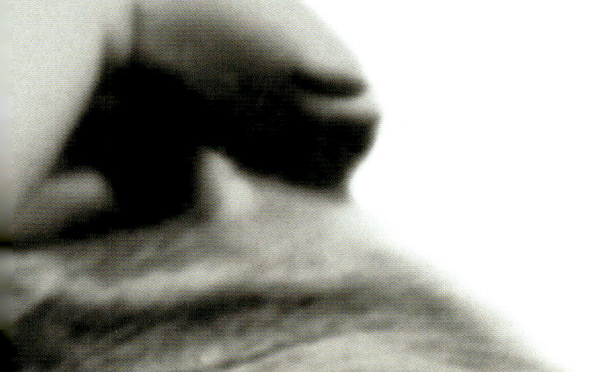

War, the Jews of Europe were a diverse and vibrant community of people. There were rich and poor, religious and secular, socialists, capitalists, professors and labourers - a broad spectrum of ordinary European people, living their lives as they had for centuries before.

The majority of Jews lived poor, humble lives in the small towns - 'Shetls' - of Central and Eastern Europe. Some, however, were educated in the language and literature of their homelands, contributing to their wealth and prosperity. Each, in their own way, contributed to the societies in which they lived, and were part of a rich tapestry of European life. These pictures were all taken between 1918 and 1943 in territories later occupied by Hitler's armies.

All were potentially victims of the Holocaust.

Some survived to tell their stories. Most did not.

'By three things is the world sustained: by justice, by truth and by peace'.

The Talmud, the Jewish book of religious law and practice, completed in the 6th Century and still used by practicing Jews today.

antisemitism

The idea of the 'Eternal Wandering Jew' depicted Jews as cursed by God to wander the earth.

Europe has not always appreciated its Jewish communities. From the early years of the Common Era (AD), Jews faced rivalry from an increasingly hostile Christian Church. By the Fourth Century the Church dictated the politics of many of the European countries where Jews were living and, more significantly, the attitudes of the people.

Christianity began as a branch of the Jewish faith and Jesus himself was a Jew. But soon, Christians began to accuse Jews of being the murderers of Christ and the enemy of the Church. Wherever Jews settled in Christian Europe, it was usually an uncomfortable if not a hostile place to be.

Jews were isolated, segregated, misunderstood and then demonised. They were subjected to Crusades in the 1100s, expelled from England in the 1200s, blamed for the Black Death in the 1300s, expelled from Spain in the 1400s, abused by Martin Luther in the 1500s, massacred in Eastern Europe in the 1600s, and driven out of Russia in the 1800s. Trades were restricted and controlled - they were forced to become money-lenders at one time and farmers at another. Judaism was misunderstood and misconstrued.

'Their synagogues should be set on fire...for the honour of Christianity... their homes should be destroyed... their rabbis forbidden to preach under threat of death... Let us drive them from the country for all time. If this advice does not suit, then find a better one that we may be rid of this devlish burden - the Jews'.

Martin Luther, German church reformer and founder of the Lutheran Church, 1543.

A Jew is depicted in this woodcut striking the crucified Christ. Jews were said to be enemies of Christ and hence, the enemies of Christians.

Jews were often depicted as being 'Judas', the betrayer of Christ.

Statues on Strasbourg cathedral: 'Ecclesia' (Christians) the church with a crown and royal sceptre and...

...blind, rejected 'Synagoga' (the Jews) with her broken staff gave a clear message to churchgoers that Jews were blind, broken and lost.

A painting portraying Shakespeare's 'Shylock', the Jew from 'The Merchant of Venice'.

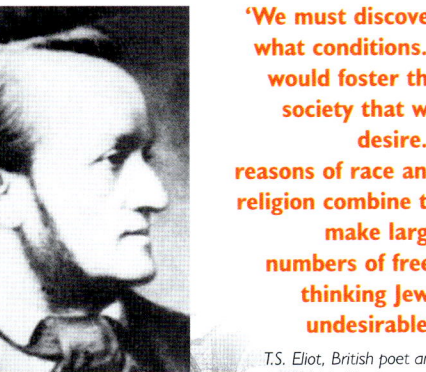

German composer Richard Wagner (1813 - 1883) supported the kinds of racist ideas that influenced the Nazis, and as well as being a fine composer he also wrote antisemitic literature which Adolf Hitler admired.

'We must discover what conditions... would foster the society that we desire... reasons of race and religion combine to make large numbers of free-thinking Jews undesirable'.

T.S. Eliot, British poet and 1948 Nobel literary prize winner, writing before the war. Even learned thinkers in Britain held antisemitic views.

In the Nineteenth Century, religious hostility and occasional violence gave way to a more sinister, modern form of antisemitism.

'Scientific Racism', social theory, centuries of religious hostility and cultural mistrust led to the repetition of hideous lies for political ends - which people all too readily believed. Instead of Jews being freer in modern society, they often found themselves the scapegoats of Europe. One publication, 'The Protocols of the Elders of Zion', was given out widely. It was supposed to show that there was a Jewish plot to control the world. It was later shown to be a fraud, started in Czarist Russia. However, this same book is still published and read in parts of the world today.

Antisemitism is a form of racism against Jewish people. It is important to understand its history for us to be effective in halting its repetition in the future.

Whether intended or not, Shakespeare's portrayal of Jews in 'The Merchant of Venice' reflected the ignorance common in his day.

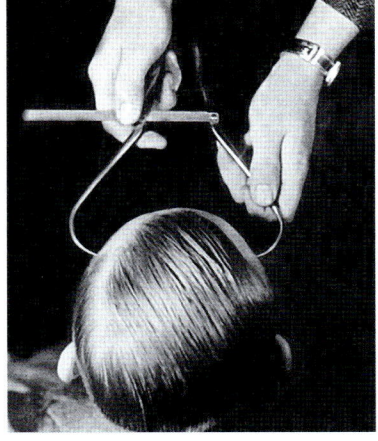

In the 19th Century, scientists began trying to determine racial superiority by examining physical features. Though misguided, Hitler later used such 'science' to demonstrate the superiority of the Aryan race as compared to the Jews and other groups.

This antisemitic cartoon from Austria states that Jews are like the drone in a hive, implying that Jews let others do all the work.

Many political parties promoted antisemitism for political gain. This campaign poster for Austria's Christian Socialists depicts a caricatured Jew in the form of a snake. It reads, 'Vote Christian Socialist, Save Austria.' (Vienna, 1920.)

The trial of Captain Alfred Dreyfus in 1894 showed the kind of antisemitism that existed in Europe. Dreyfus was blamed for an error of the French counter-intelligence service, and sentenced to life imprisonment. It took ten years before he was pardoned. The whole episode showed how acceptable it was to use Jews as scapegoats. The author Emile Zola wrote an open letter to the French President, entitled 'J'Accuse', defending Dreyfus. Zola was also tried for libel.

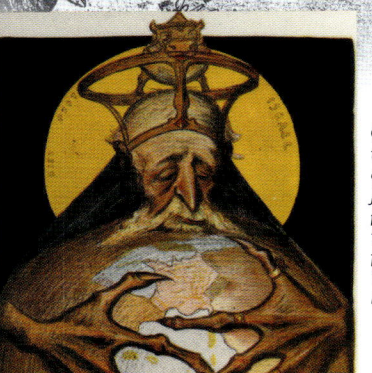

Cartoon implying that the Jews controlled the world. Jews were particularly thought to control world finance. These were misguided myths.

The Rise of Hitler

NATIONAL SOCIALISM

Hitler (left) photographed in the trenches during World War I.

A formal portrait of Hitler from the mid 1920s.

In 1918 Germany lost the First World War. The Versailles Treaty, which followed, placed heavy burdens on the German people at a time when the humiliation of defeat had already been a bitter blow.

Among the disappointed war veterans was Adolf Hitler. After fighting in the war, he worked for the German army, spying on new political parties. He ultimately joined one of these in September 1919. In 1921 he became the leader of the National Socialist German Workers Party - the Nazis. In November 1923, his party tried to take control of the regional government in Bavaria in what became known as the 'Munich Putsch'. They failed, and Hitler was sent to prison, where he served nine months of a five year sentence. There he wrote his political manifesto, one of the most infamous works of all time - 'Mein Kampf' ('My Struggle'). After his release, Hitler continued to work even more aggressively towards the ultimate power he wanted to gain.

In 1925, few would have guessed that eight years later this obscure extremist would become Chancellor of Germany.

'...a pestilence, worse than the Black Death of olden times, and the people are being infected by it...'
Hitler talking about the Jews; 'Mein Kampf', 1924.

Hitler seen celebrating the outbreak of World War I, Munich 1914. He spent four years fighting for Germany.

The Storm Troopers - the SA - were an important part of Hitler's developing power.

The SS - an elite force developed as a personal bodyguard for Hitler. They were later to become an important part of enforcing racial policy.

The Swastika - an icon of power, and a symbol of fear to those who became the victims of the Nazis.

In the Grunewald stadium; Berlin, 1933.

President von Hindenburg (left) appointed Hitler Chancellor of the Weimar Republic in January 1933. Von Hindenburg remained President until his death in August 1934. Hitler finally assumed total control of Germany at that point.

Nazi parade.

These stamps illustrate the rampant inflation prior to the Munich Putsch in November 1923.

Since the end of the First World War, Germany had been known as the Weimar Republic. This period was characterised by economic hardship and political tension.

In February 1933, the Reichstag - the parliament building - burned down. The Communists were blamed for this, and in March Hitler initiated the 'Enabling Act', transferring decision-making to the Cabinet.

WEIMAR CRISIS

This was made worse when in 1929 the stock market on Wall Street, New York, crashed and worldwide economic depression set in. In their haste to address these domestic problems, many members of the German public chose to ignore or even to believe Hitler's violent antisemitic ideas.

The Nazi party gained more and more power. By 1932 they were the largest single party, with over 37 per cent of the German population voting for them. In January 1933, Hitler took virtual control of the government when he was appointed Chancellor by President von Hindenburg.

Germany was now almost entirely under the total control of Hitler. The democracy of the Weimar Republic was soon to be dismantled, as Hitler quickly sought ways to strengthen his own power. This he did partly by persuasion, and partly by force.

'Even before Adolf Hitler came to power in 1933, the Nazis were making life uncomfortable for the Jewish population... There were unofficial boycotts and attacks on Jewish shops with worrying frequency'.

Paul Oppenheimer, a survivor of Bergen-Belsen, describing what he saw as a young boy in Berlin.

The Third Reich

Hitler wasted no time consolidating his power. Within months, all political parties except for the NSDAP had been banned; concentration camps were constructed, opponents were arrested en masse and the media was brought under state control.

Nazi ideology, with racial purity as its central theme, was extended into every aspect and level of society. Schoolbooks were rewritten and teachers took an oath of loyalty to Adolf Hitler. The 'racial sciences' exalted the Germans as the master race and reviled Jews as utterly evil. All institutions of society became servants of the regime. The Church, the judicial system, the education system, science and the arts were all controlled and used to influence and maintain the newly imposed order.

Membership of the Hitler Youth organisations became compulsory in 1936. German youth was educated 'in the spirit of National Socialism' - a mixture of entertainment, sport and propaganda.

For many Germans the benefits of National Socialism were clear; the rearmament and road building programmes were improving the economy. The propaganda campaign offered a bright and prosperous future, and restored a sense of national pride.

There is much debate about where Hitler learned his antisemitic ideas. One thing is for certain: they were not new, but he refined them and made them more accessible to wider audiences than ever before.

> 'Hitler - so we had heard on all sides - Hitler would help the fatherland to achieve greatness, fortune, and prosperity... We found this good, and were willing to do all that we could to contribute to the common effort.'
>
> Inge Scholl, writing in her book 'The White Rose'.

This book was used by children in Germany. They collected picture cards for it about the story of the Nazis. It glorified the party and its beliefs, and is one example of propaganda made attractive for young people.

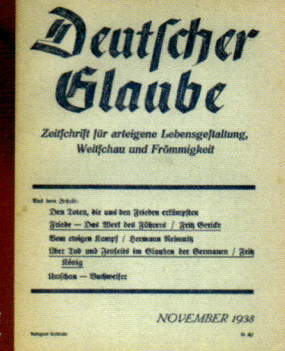

'Deutscher Glaube' - German belief - was a monthly publication instructing the clergy in Nazi Germany about what to preach, making Christianity virtually a Nazi religion.

Girls, in the League of German Girls, take part in exercises. To belong to this was a part of life - unless you were Jewish.

Adolf Hitler believed that young people were the future of a loyal Nazi state.

German women enjoy a Nazi rally.

'Even the old adore the Führer.' Taken from a propaganda picture.

There were two strands involved in the development of Nazi ideology. The first was based on German mythology. It looked back to a rural way of life. The Nazis spoke of the 'one-nation community'.

The other main strand was that of scientific racism, and racial hygiene. Scientific racism was widespread throughout the western world. Racial hygiene was an attempt to impose scientific racism through government policy.

To maintain the balance of power, Hitler developed a complex governmental structure, with his own supremacy unchallengeable. In 1934 he curbed the strength of the SA, ordering the assassination of their leader Ernst Röhm, his only possible challenger. The 4.5 million members of the SA then came fully under Hitler's control.

As early as 1924 Hitler had as his bodyguards a dedicated protection squad - the SS. After the SA were crushed, the SS came to play a key role in enforcing Hitler's objectives. Along with the SD (the Security Service) they maintained tight control within the Reich, and later, in its occupied territories. Reichsführer-SS, Heinrich Himmler, had control of the activities of the SS and secret police - the Gestapo.

"**The adoration that the German people had for Hitler had to be seen to be believed. I can remember some of the streets actually being full of roses and carnations, strewn the whole width of the street for his car. They adored him; absolutely adored him.**"

Lisa Vincent. A Jewish refugee from Nuremberg, Adolf Hitler's favourite Bavarian city.

The Volkswagen Beetle and the Autobahn (motorway) became symbols of Nazi success.

Josef Goebbels, Nazi Minister for Propaganda

The Lebensborn programme. Children deemed racially pure were nurtured for the Nazi state in a special Nazi nursery.

The Third Reich

Circumstances for the Jewish community deteriorated rapidly. Initially, violent measures were sporadic. Then, on 1 April 1933, a boycott of Jewish businesses was initiated. Windows of shops were daubed with slogans, and Storm Troopers prevented non-Jews from entering.

A week later, the civil service law was passed, dismissing all non-Aryans from the civil service and teaching professions. This was the first of hundreds of pieces of legislation isolating Jews from society. The process of discrimination against the Jews developed over a period of time. Boycotts of Jewish businesses and restrictions on education soon gave way to restrictions in public places, with signs placed to indicate forbidden areas.

In 1935, the Nuremberg laws stated who was a Jew according to Nazi definition. All people born of at least one Jewish grandparent were now singled out for discrimination. Jews living in Germany lost their right to citizenship at this time.

In 1937, all Jewish property was registered. In 1938 the remaining few Jewish businesses were 'Aryanised'. In July 1938, Jewish doctors were forbidden to treat non-Jews; in September, Jewish lawyers were forbidden to practice; in October, passports were marked with a letter 'J' for 'Jude' (Jew). In August 1938, all Jewish women were to take the middle name 'Sara', and Jewish men the name 'Israel'.

In 1938, passports were marked with a letter 'J' for Jude - Jew. All Jewish women were to take the middle name 'Sara', and Jewish men the name 'Israel'.

Park bench; the sign reads 'For Aryans only'. Jews were excluded from using public transport and from visiting the cinema or theatre. Step by step, Jews were removed from society.

'Wherever books will be burned, men also, in the end, are burned.'
Heinrich Heine, a German Jewish poet. From his work 'Almansor', 1823.

In May 1933, Dr Goebbels organised bonfires around Germany to burn books by authors deemed not to fit in with the Nazi viewpoint. SA and students took part, burning literature from prominent Jewish and political writers such as Sigmund Freud, Thomas Mann and Karl Marx.

A Jewish boy, in school, is made to stand in front of the class while the teacher 'informs' the class about the Jews. The text on the board reads: 'The Jews are our enemy. Beware of the Jews.'

The night after Kristallnacht, 10 November 1938. German citizens stand across the road and watch a Jewish man pick through the debris of his possessions. By this time the Nazis are so well entrenched, it appears, that no-one is prepared to cross the street to help the man clear up. They simply stand and watch.

A web of legislation had been spun to trap a now fearful Jewish community, who found it difficult to leave, and even more difficult to stay.

Those who could leave did so. For those who stayed, discrimination was to turn into violent attacks.

In November 1938 a Jewish student in Paris named Herschel Grynszpan, angry at the way his parents had been treated in Germany, shot a German diplomat.

Two days later, on 9 November, Josef Goebbels used the incident as an excuse to organise a nationwide riot against the Jews. The SA organised the rioting, while the Gestapo and SS made summary arrests of Jewish men. During the rampage, Jewish homes, businesses and synagogues were destroyed. The tragic

Street scene after Kristallnacht, the Night of Broken Glass.

'It must have been three or four o'clock in the morning when I was ripped out of my sleep by the sound of smashing crockery and glass... They rushed about the room smashing, throwing, trampling. Now fear became a living thing'.

Hannule Zurndorfen, writing in her book 'The Ninth of November'.

event left the pavements of Germany's cities covered in shattered glass and debris. Some 91 Jews were killed and over 30,000 were detained in concentration camps.

This night of violence is seen as a turning point in Nazi policy. The full extent of their hatred had now been demonstrated. It became known as 'Kristallnacht': the Night of Broken Glass.

A destroyed synagogue, November 1938.

The Union Jack and Swastika fly together above the hotel where the Munich agreement was made.

The road to War

Hitler was determined to win Lebensraum, `Living Space', for the German people. This was needed, he said, to satisfy their economic requirements and prove their racial superiority over other nations.

Three days after becoming Chancellor, Hitler addressed his top generals and admirals, outlining his rearmament intentions in direct defiance of the Versailles Treaty. This was the beginning of a catalogue of treaty violations that over the next six years led Europe down the road to war.

In 1935, the people of the Saarland - under French control since the Treaty - voted decisively to return to Germany. Britain's policy towards Germany at this time was one of appeasement, giving concessions to keep the peace. In 1935, Britain signed the Anglo-German Naval Agreement, which relaxed armament restrictions on Germany. The policy of appeasement, it is now understood, allowed Hitler more time to ready himself for war.

In 1936, Hitler marched into the land west of the River Rhine. The Allies, avoiding conflict and overestimating Hitler's military strength at the time, did nothing. Later that year, Hitler and Mussolini established an alliance which would be formalised in 1939 as the 'Pact of Steel'.

In March 1938, Hitler marched into Austria and was welcomed as a hero. This was known as the Anschluss. The secret police rounded up anyone who resisted. In a referendum, following the Anschluss, 99% of Austrians voted to unite with Germany. The Allies made only verbal protests.

British Prime Minister signs the Munich Pact in September 1938, allowing Hitler's Germany to claim the Sudeten region of Czechoslovakia in return for peace.

"My good friends, this is the second time in our history that there has come back from Germany to Downing Street peace with honour. I believe it is peace in our time."

British Prime Minister, Neville Chamberlain.

At the Evian conference in July 1938, delegates from 32 countries gathered to discuss the problem of Jewish refugees. Sadly, they did little to help and the Jews were trapped.

937 Jewish refugees set sail aboard the St Louis. After they were refused entry to Cuba, they were not wanted in America and so returned to Europe. Many perished in the Holocaust.

German troops entering Poland, 1 September 1939.

Hitler's next demand was the area of Czechoslovakia adjacent to Germany, containing mainly German-speaking people - the Sudetenland. British Prime Minister Neville Chamberlain, who described Czechoslovakia as "a far-off land of which we know nothing", called for talks, and a conference was held in Munich on 29 September 1938 between Adolf Hitler, Neville Chamberlain, Benito Mussolini and Eduard Daladier of France.

Hitler was allowed to occupy the Sudetenland. Chamberlain returned to London, declaring "peace in our time". Hitler described the Munich agreement as "an undreamed-of triumph". By March 1939, he had occupied Prague itself. The policy of appeasement was by now a complete failure.

Hitler's next move was most likely to be Poland. The Allies opened talks with the Russians, but on 22 August 1939, Hitler announced a Non-Aggression Pact with Stalin. Armed with this guarantee, ten days later, Hitler invaded Poland.

After Kristallnacht, refuge was offered in Great Britain to some 10,000 children whose parents wished to send their children off the European mainland for safety. Many of the children who were sent to England were Jewish children escaping Germany. They were all placed with families in Britain; some with Jewish families, others not. The children thought that their stay in England would be temporary, and that once the trouble had died down they would return to their parents.

Most of the children never saw their parents again. The experience of children who were refugees or were hidden during the war is often overlooked because they were not in the camps. They, too, were victims of the Nazis. They, too, escaped otherwise certain death.

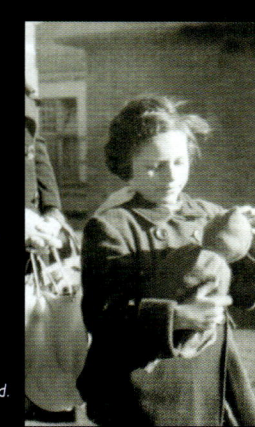

Vera Schaufeld.

a gathering storm

After the invasion of Poland in September 1939, a village is burned to the ground while ethnic Germans observe.

'I remember waving furiously out of the window. My mother was crying. I never saw her again.'

Vera Schaufeld, aged 9.

The First Step: Ghettos

In September 1939, the Nazis devised a plan to round up the Jews of Poland and relocate them into areas known as ghettos. Several hundred ghettos were established in Poland alone. Later, when the Nazis invaded further European countries, similar ghettos were established.

Walls and fences were erected around most ghetto areas. The Nazis operated a policy of overcrowding, starvation and degradation. The reason why they did this is still unclear, but it is known that they had a 'final aim', which may have been either the deportation or the mass murder of the Jews.

A council of Jewish elders was appointed to run each ghetto. The council was responsible for food distribution, welfare and the application of Nazi law to the ghetto population. They also had to select people suitable to work and, eventually, to assist in deporting Jews.

Life in the ghetto became increasingly difficult. To begin with it was possible for the population to maintain a sense of normality. There were bars and theatres and concerts. As soon as resources became more scarce, life in the ghettos became a fight for survival.

Thousands of people started to die as conditions deteriorated. Food was in desperately short supply and children often took on the role of smuggling food from outside the ghetto to help their families to live.

Slave labourers were taken from among the population of the ghettos to help with the German war effort. These individuals were worked hard with no pay and little food. Work did mean that for a short period, a person's value to the Nazis might prevent his or her deportation to harsher conditions in the concentration camps.

Survival became a form of resistance to the Nazis. Jews adopted a determination to survive the obvious policy to slowly kill off the ghetto population through starvation, disease and work. People continued to smuggle, to learn, to pray and to plan for the future.

Deportations from the ghettos began in 1942. The Nazis had established their plan to murder all Jews without exception, and transports left the ghettos of Europe virtually every day for the death camps. Worn down, and believing the lies about their safety, the Jews had no option but to board the trains to certain death.

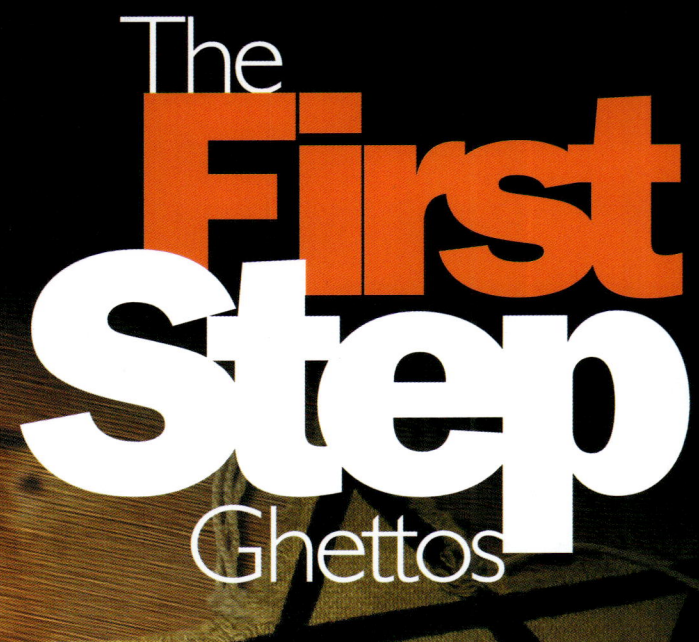

Stars of David were enforced in the ghettos

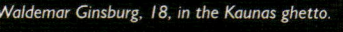

'The barbed wire was completed, the guards in position, and the gate shut. We were trapped. From then on we were fully occupied coping with the atrocious conditions, the overcrowding and the hunger'.

Waldemar Ginsburg, 18, in the Kaunas ghetto.

Jews entering the Lodz ghetto. The sign reads: 'Living area of the Jews. Trespassing is forbidden.'

Movement of Jews in the Warsaw ghetto.

Performance in the Warsaw ghetto Jewish theatre.

Selling bread in the Warsaw ghetto.

Boys in the Warsaw ghetto. There were many orphans in the ghetto, as adults often died first.

Lone children huddle in a doorway; the Warsaw ghetto.

Young boy collecting bodies, Warsaw ghetto.

Orphaned children died on the streets of the ghettos every day.

Newspaper boy sells the daily paper, the Jewish Gazette.

'Foraging was often done by children, since the risk was greater for adults. I regularly took off my yellow star and went over to the 'Aryan' side... I was caught and beaten black-and-blue more than once'.

Kitty Hart-Moxon, who was in the Lublin ghetto, aged 12.

Mass murder

Girls posing in Eisiskes, Lithuania. A year after this photograph was taken, all the Jews in this village were killed by the Einsatzgruppen. Photo: Courtesy of The Yaffa Eliach Shtetl Collection.

On 22 June 1941, the German army invaded the Soviet Union. In this territory there lived around 3.5 million Jews.

Following behind the German army were special groups of SS personnel called the Einsatzgruppen. Their task was to go into the towns and villages, round up people and kill them. Their main victims were Jews - men, women and children. They also targeted other 'enemies of the Reich' including partisans, Communists and Gypsies.

Jewish families were taken from their homes and shot into mass graves in the forests or ravines. Ordinary soldiers of the Wehrmacht - the regular army - often assisted the SS. The Einsatzgruppen were responsible for the ruthless murder of over one million people, mainly Jews. Thousands of communities that had existed for centuries were systematically destroyed as these death squads swept through.

The operation which was started by the Einsatzgruppen in June 1941 was a new phase in Nazi policy towards the Jews. It can be seen as the beginning of the 'Final Solution of the Jewish Question'. The total annihilation of the Jewish people was now being attempted by the Nazis, as forecast by Hitler in his Reichstag speech of January 1939, two-and-a-half years earlier.

When the Nazis invaded Lithuania, a tragic feature of the mass murder was the collaboration of the local militia. They saw the Nazis as liberators from Communist oppression, and murdered their fellow Lithuanians as 'Jewish Bolsheviks'. The same situation was echoed in some other East European countries, such as Latvia and the Ukraine. For countries previously occupied by the Communists, the Nazis were seen by some to be liberators from Communism. This made these people more ready to assist the Nazis.

'The next day sixty Jews were herded into a garage forecourt for forced labour. When the work was finished, the militia started a new bout of beatings, using crow-bars, spades and rifles. Many were killed on the spot'.
Waldemar Ginsburg.

Lithuanian collaborators murder Lithuanian Jews, Kaunas, 1941.

No one was spared. Women and children, considered to be subhuman, were a threat; they would produce another generation capable of infecting the pure German race.

Jews forced to dig their own grave.

'As this war is in our opinion a Jewish war, the Jews are the first to feel it. Here in Russia, wherever the German soldier is, no Jew remains'.
SS Obersturmführer Karl Kretschmer, writing to his wife in September 1942.

TASK FORCE*

* a literal translation of "Einsatzgruppen"

```
Berlin July 19, 1941

Einsatzgruppe C:

Locale: Zhitomir

Zhitomir had a population of
90,000, of which 30% were Jews,
15% Poles, the rest Ukranians
and about 4,000 ethnic Germans.

Now approximately 40,000 remain.
```

Each unit which was involved in mass killings had to file regular reports. Many of these still exist. From these reports you can see clearly just what large numbers of people were being murdered. In Zhitomir some 50,000 people were murdered by the Einsatzgruppen.

It is always difficult to understand what motivated Germans and their collaborators to do such things. It remains a dilemma to know whether they specifically hated Jews and wanted to kill them, or whether they were ordinary people caught up in the evil of the Nazi regime.

If they were just ordinary men and women, the question is whether, today, we would behave in a similar way in similar circumstances.

This photograph was found in the personal album of a soldier, entitled, 'The Last Jew of Vinnitsa'. There were 28,000 Jews living in Vinnitsa before the Nazis arrived.

The 'Final

In their attempt to find a solution to what antisemites of the previous century called the 'Jewish Question', the Nazis took extreme measures. Their racial policies took priority over everything. First they tried to isolate the Jews from society and force them to emigrate. When this failed, they decided on what they termed the Endlösung - the 'Final Solution' of the Jewish Question. This meant total annihilation of the Jews of Europe. Every man, woman and child was to be murdered.

No-one knows when the decision was made to destroy all the Jews, but when the ghettos were established, Heydrich spoke about them being 'one step towards the final aim'. Certainly by the middle of 1941, preparations were being made for the implementation of this catastrophic policy.

The Einsatzgruppen were responsible for murdering well over a million people after the invasion of the Soviet Union in June 1941. This method of killing was considered too slow by the Nazi leadership. They were also concerned about the effects it had on the soldiers and SS taking part in the shooting. This was when gassing methods were developed.

A conference about the 'Final Solution' took

Jews are loaded onto cattle wagons. They are told they will be resettled, but are taken to one of the death camps in Poland where they will be murdered.

Jews aboard cattle wagons about to leave for one of the death camps from Westerbork, a transit camp in Holland.

Waiting in line after disembarking. These women with children will be selected for the gas chambers.

Arriving from Hungary at Auschwitz-Birkenau. They had been told, and probably believed, that they have come to be resettled.

Prisoners load up the belongings of the new arrivals on trucks, to take them for sorting in the 'Kanada' section of Auschwitz-Birkenau.

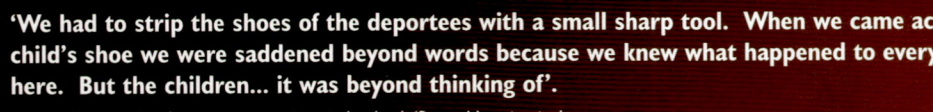

'We had to strip the shoes of the deportees with a small sharp tool. When we came across a child's shoe we were saddened beyond words because we knew what happened to everyone here. But the children... it was beyond thinking of'.

Victoria Vincent, Auschwitz survivor, writing in her book 'Beyond Imagination'.

Poster found in one of the camps, quoting from a speech made in the Reichstag by Hitler before the war in January 1939. It reads:

"If the international Jewish financiers once again start a World War...the result will be the annihilation of the Jews in Europe."

This speech was widely heard and read, but no one imagined that within a few years the Nazis would fulfil this promise.

Solution'

...lace at Wannsee (a suburb of Berlin) in January 1942. ...s purpose was to inform government officials of their ...le in the destruction of the Jews. Their aim was to ...ill all 11 million Jews throughout Europe, including the ...30,000 living in England.

One of the concerning aspects of this whole ...agedy is how ordinary people in society became ...volved, either directly, or as facilitators of this systematic mass murder of their fellow human beings.

In Auschwitz and Majdanek, selections of the new arrivals took place when transports arrived. Around 75 per cent went straight to the gas chamber. The others were reprieved from immediate death, and taken for work as slave labourers. Most died from the severe conditions within months.

There were four other death camps in Poland solely for the purpose of killing; Belzec, Chelmno, Sobibor and Treblinka. Apart from a handful of prisoners used to maintain these camps and work in their crematoria, all the others were gassed on arrival. The pictures on these pages show one transport of Jews arriving in Auschwitz-Birkenau. They were taken by an SS photographer.

...oes of the new arrivals at Auschwitz were sorted by inmates assigned to the 'Schuhkommando'.

Children, considered no use for labour, were selected for immediate death. Here they are walking towards one of the crematoria at Birkenau.

Child waiting with family next to the gas chambers and crematoria. They clearly do not realise where they are or what fate awaits them.

Transport of Hungarian Jews on the 'ramp' at Auschwitz-Birkenau. They stand in queues after a terrible journey in the closed cattle wagons. They undergo selection. About 25 per cent will be selected for labour - they will be worked to death under harsh conditions. All the others - children, women with children, pregnant women, the old and infirm, will be led straight to the gas chamber, where they will be murdered within hours of arrival. The column in the background is walking towards one of the crematoria.

There were four gas chambers at Auschwitz-Birkenau, with crematoria similar to this being built here. A further crematorium was sited at Auschwitz' main camp.

'There was not enough room to lie down in the barracks, where there were 1200 women. We slept in rows, back to back, with knees pulled up and feet touching. Many of us had dysentery, and climbing over bodies to get out made some women scream, causing the guards to shoot into the barrack'.

Trude Levi, Auschwitz survivor.

The Camp System

The infamous gateway to Birkenau. In the later stages of the camp's operation, trains passed through here from all over Europe to the 'ramp', where the deportees were unloaded ready for the selection.

> 'I remember the day our transport arrived at Auschwitz-Birkenau. The wagons were opened and the people ordered out. The scenes I observed were just too terrifying to imagine'.
>
> Arek Hersh, survivor.

The Nazis developed a system of camps in order to enforce their rule of terror, first of all in Germany. They repeated this in the other countries of Europe that they occupied. But there were different camps for different functions. The first were established within weeks of the Nazis coming to power, as detention centres to hold their political opponents. The first concentration camp to be built was at Dachau, near Munich, in March 1933. Communists, socialists and trade unionists were put here; anyone who opposed the Nazi way of thinking.

In many of the camps the treatment was so harsh that thousands died from cruelty, hunger, disease and random executions. The inmates were roused early in the morning for 'roll call', where they would stand in rows in all weather, sometimes for hours on end, while they were repeatedly counted to make sure everyone was there.

Although loss of life was expected in these camps, and crematoria were built to deal with the dead, gas chambers were only constructed in six camps in Poland to systematically murder the Jews. They did not start operating until after December 1941 and within three years over four million people, mainly Jews, had been murdered in these places.

There were also transit camps, mainly in Western Europe, which were used to collect prisoners before deportation. Usually, this destination was 'East' to one of the death camps in Poland.

Some camps did not fit into a particular category; for instance Theresienstadt, or Terezin, near Prague. This was used to fool the Western world that the Jews were being settled into Jewish towns. Although it had many features of a ghetto, in reality, Terezin acted like a transit camp: most people were soon put onto transports 'East' where they were murdered.

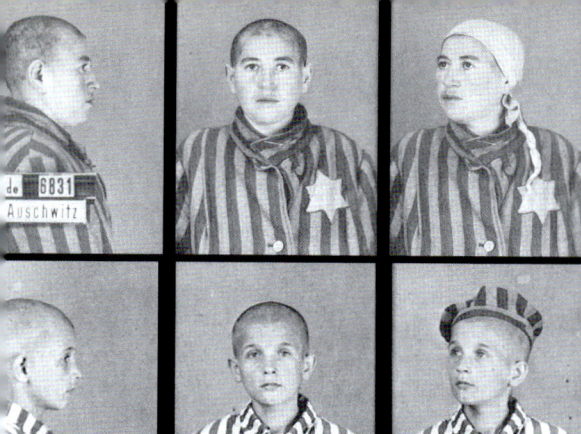

On arrival in the camps, inmates were shaved, their clothes and belongings were taken from them and they were usually given ill-fitting camp clothes.

Heinrich Himmler was responsible for the concentration camp system and the training of the SS. He oversaw the development of the machinery of mass destruction.

Prisoners were utilised for slave labour. Conditions varied in different camps, but few prisoners survived more than a few months.

In labour camps, most inmates were used for slave labour. There was a policy of 'death through work'. Even though this work may have been useful for the German war effort, their lives were expendable as far as the Nazis were concerned. When they could no longer perform useful work, they would be taken to the gas chambers after one of the many 'selections' that took place.

As well as the maintenance work, road building and quarrying that the prisoners were made to do for the SS, many large German companies made use of their labour. Sometimes the inmates were marched out of the camps, through towns to private factories. Some of the industries were vast, such as the multimillion pound consortium IG Farben, which established a rubber works near Auschwitz.

It was only with the creation of the 'Final Solution' that the six death camps were introduced, whose principle aim was the murder of men, women and children in the most organised and efficient way possible. There had been concentration camps and labour camps in history before. Never before however, had there been camps created solely to destroy human life.

Map of Poland, showing the six death camps in red.

'I don't know how to describe hunger, not the type everybody is familiar with when a meal has been skipped, but hunger that causes actual pain; or what it is like to be cold without the prospect of ever becoming warm again'.

Anita Lasker-Wallfisch, Auschwitz survivor, writing in 'Inherit the Truth'.

Hungarian women 'admitted' to a camp: shaved, numbered, and given only flimsy clothes for the severe weather of Eastern Europe. Many of these women will die within months.

Gypsy prisoners, Dachau.

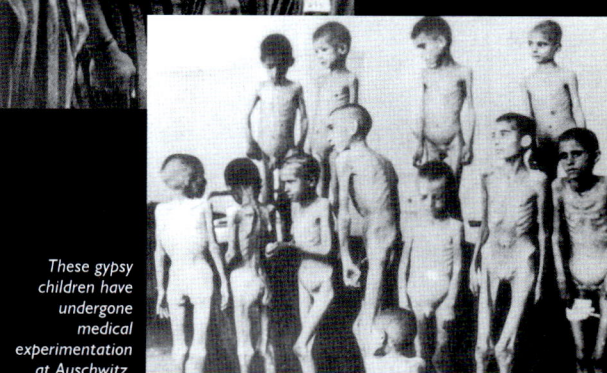

These gypsy children have undergone medical experimentation at Auschwitz.

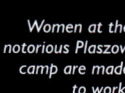

Women at the notorious Plaszow camp are made to work.

'We have rejected the German ultimatum urging us to surrender, because the enemy, knowing no mercy, leaves us no alternative. As time runs out, we demand that you remember how we've been betrayed; there will come a day of reckoning for our sacred, spilt blood'.

Mordechai Anielewicz, resistance leader, writing on 28 April 1943.

Little could be done to stop the advance of the Nazi army or halt the terror campaign. However, there were Jews who took the initiative, through a number of means, to resist the Nazi intent to destroy them en masse.

Ghetto fighters took on the Nazis in a number of ghettos including Warsaw, Bialystok and Vilnius. In Warsaw, the Jews held out for several weeks. Partisans based in Eastern Europe waged a guerrilla war in the forests of Belarus and Lithuania. Sabotage, strikes and propaganda campaigns were waged underground wherever possible. Even espionage activities, to inform on Nazi policy, were undertaken at great personal risk. Hiding places were created by families, and many people attempted to escape into the forests.

It should be understood that the very will to survive and continue life in the face of such hostility was itself resistance to the tide of destruction. For many Jews, survival was the greatest act of resistance as everything the Nazis did was designed to murder them.

Partisans demonstrate sabotage of a railway line.

From 1942 to the war's end, Ukrainians Stepan and Olga Dragan hid nine Jews in a bunker beneath their kitchen, only 100 metres from the local Gestapo HQ. A partisan, Stepan was shot by collaborators after the war was over.

A defiant Jewish woman is rounded up by the SS while taking part in the Warsaw ghetto uprising.

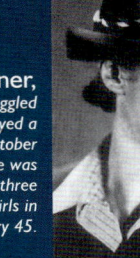

Ala Gartner, *held at Auschwitz, smuggled explosives which destroyed a crematorium in the October '44 uprising. She was publicly hanged with three other girls in January 45.*

Hannah Senesh *joined the RAF and was dropped behind enemy lines. She tried to warn the Jews but was caught and executed in Budapest, 1944.*

Hesia Strom *was a partisan from Kaunas, Lithuania. She fought with a partisan unit in the Rudnicki forest south of Vilnius.*

Sophie Scholl *and her brother, Hans, began a German resistance movement in 1942 known as the White Rose. They distributed anti-Nazi leaflets. Both were caught and executed.*

RESISTANCE

The Courage to care

They all have one thing in common; they were prepared to risk everything in order to save a life

During the Holocaust, many millions of individuals were murdered because of who they were. Sadly, few were rescued from their impending fate. There were, however, a relatively small number of non-Jewish people who recognised what was happening to the Jews of Europe and were prepared to risk their lives in order to try and save others, or oppose the Nazi regime.

A few of them have been mentioned on this page. Thousands more are remembered at the Avenue of the Righteous in Yad Vashem in Jerusalem.

Some saved thousands of lives by helping people escape; others hid a smaller number, a family or an individual.

They all have one thing in common; they were prepared to risk everything in order to save a life.

Raoul Wallenberg
ish diplomat who saved thousands of Jews in Hungary by issuing passes.

Gita Bauer,
who hid her Jewish friend. "What else could I say but 'I'll take you into my home'? There was no big moral or religious decision. She was a friend and needed help."

Varian Fry
American who rescued thousands from France with his team based in Marseilles.

Oscar Schindler
took over one thousand Jewish prisoners from Krakow to his factory, protecting them from almost certain death.

Helena Melnyczuk
A Ukrainian, with her Catholic father and brother, she hid their former Jewish neighbours who escaped the ghetto.

Sempo Sugihara
ruined his political career in Japan when he was the ambassador in Kaunas. He issued thousands of visas allowing Jews to escape to the Far East.

Nearly all of Denmark's 8,000 Jews were rescued by the underground when the Nazis planned to deport them. Most were eventually ferried to safety in Sweden in fishing boats.

'I looked at all those people clinging to the iron fences of the consulate begging for visas, and I thought I just had to do something for them. In pure joy, they would fall to their knees in thanks. I was so inspired by the sight that I worked non-stop for a month writing visas'.

Sempo Sugihara, Japanese Consul in Lithuania.

a spectrum of

Although the 'Final Solution' was aimed at destroying the Jewish communities of Europe, there were other victims of this Nazi terror. The disabled were targeted in a euthanasia programme. They were considered to be racially inferior, and an economic burden on the state. Over 70,000 were murdered between 1939 and 1941. Slavic people were said by the Nazis to be inferior to the German Aryans. As such, they were not systematically murdered, but millions of Poles died from executions and mistreatment. Many were taken for use as slave labour. Several million Soviet prisoners of war died, mostly due to deliberate starvation and exposure to cold in the camps. Homosexuals were also targeted by the Nazis. Many died as prisoners in the camp system.

Jehovah's Witnesses, like the people in the photo on the left, were interned from an early stage of the camp system, for refusing to acknowledge Hitler as the supreme leader. The Roma and Sinti people - the Gypsies - were treated as subhuman by the Nazis. Although Nazi policy towards them was somewhat confused in the early years, eventually, like the Jews, they were subject to mass murder; approximately 500,000 were killed. Many were shot by the Einsatzgruppen, and thousands were killed in the gas chambers at Auschwitz.

Victor and Mary Schnell, Jehovah's Witnesses, married in 1948. Victor survived Auschwitz; Mary survived the Stutthof concentration camp.

victims

1, Helen Gotthold. A Jehovah's Witness, she was tried and executed for her anti-Nazi views.

2, Helen Gotthold with her children, Gerd and Gisela.

3, Rosalia Makula from the nomadic Lovari Gypsy clan.

4, A 'race expert' with Gypsies.

5, Cemetery at the Hadamar Euthanasia facility.

6, Smoke rises from the crematorium at Hadamar.

7, A head physician at the Kaufbeuren Euthanasia facility.

8, Buses at Hadamar. Such buses were adapted to gas 'patients' with carbon monoxide.

9, A caravan of Gypsies, Czechoslovakia, 1938.

10, A Gypsy youth from the nomadic Lovari (horse trading) clan.

As the Germans retreated from Eastern Europe, they left the concentration camps and took any inmates that could still walk with them. They marched tens of thousands of prisoners across hundreds of miles on what became known as death marches. By this time the prisoners were starving, diseased and very weak. The winter of 1944-1945 was a bitterly cold one and the prisoners were walking through freezing temperatures, often sleeping in the snow outside. There was virtually no food and no shelter. As a result of this mistreatment, prisoners fell by the roadside and either were left to die, or were shot by the SS guards who were escorting them.

death marches

The prisoners were forced to walk or were put on to trains and sent right into German territory to other concentration camps or factories. Thousands died en route, more died on arrival, and yet more died in the last few months of the war while they waited and hoped that the Allies would arrive. As they waited, the overcrowding in the concentration camps became worse, food supplies became more scarce and disease began to spread more and more rapidly. In the two months prior to liberation, almost 35,000 people died at Bergen-Belsen alone.

'The death march began. The method was designed to cause anguish and inflict pain. Five of us abreast and SS on both sides. We were all running and being beaten practically all the time. Anybody who fell and did not rise quickly enough was shot. People were falling like flies'.
Harry Ernstoff, writing in 'No Thanks for the Memories'.

Liberation
the pain of survival

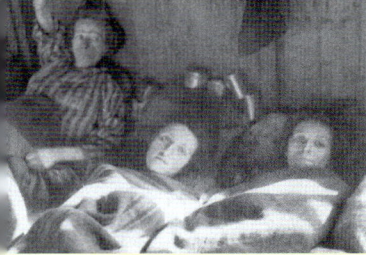

Soviet officials discovered 700kg of hair in bales in the Auschwitz stores. There were also shoes, clothes and personal effects awaiting transport to the Reich.

Even after liberation, thousands died from disease and malnutrition.

The things their eyes have seen ...
Girl liberated from Bergen-Belsen.

The British made the captured SS carry their victims to mass graves.

Their homes, families and communities gone, many stayed in the camps for over a year after liberation as 'displaced persons'.

A liberated prisoner; free, but where to go?

Towards the end of 1944, Allied forces were making considerable progress deep into German-occupied territory and Germany itself. Russian troops were the first to discover the extent of the Nazi atrocities when they liberated camps in Poland in late 1944.

By early 1945, British and American troops were pressing into Germany from the West, and made swift advances throughout March. On 11 April 1945, American forces discovered the concentration camp at Buchenwald and found things worse than they had seen throughout the whole war.

At Nuremberg in 1945, the Allies put some of the Nazi leaders on trial. Some were sentenced to death; many, however, received prison sentences of only a few years.

"I had many illusions when I was liberated. I thought ... that generations to come would be free from prejudice forever. Alas, I was wrong".
Anita Lasker-Wallfisch, Bergen-Belsen, 15 April, 1945.

Holocaust survivor Arek Hersh stands by one of the mass graves containing the family he left behind in a church at Sieradz, aged twelve.

forgotten places

Zbylitowska Gora: The entrance to a mass grave, dedicated to the memory of the eight hundred children who were murdered here.

Memorial Stone at Treblinka, where over eight hundred thousand Jews were murdered in less than a year.

In June 1942, six thousand Jews were taken and shot dead in woodland near the town of Tarnow. Among them that day were 800 children. Should you go there today, there is a peaceful woodland, where green grass covers their mass graves. Few people know who is buried in these woods, and few really care. No-one knows who those children were, they have no names, no faces, and no-one to remember them. Who can remember what they were like, what personalities they had, their hopes and dreams? The memory of those 800 children is forever lost. Like all of the 1,500,000 children killed by the Nazis, their lives are no more than figures on a page. They inhabit the many forgotten places of the Holocaust, where thousands of lives were lost without trace.

Going to these forgotten places of the Holocaust, we can see that we have a duty to remember what happened, where and to whom. We have to learn the facts. We also need to learn about the people whose lives the facts are about. Today, if you go to the towns and villages where many Jewish communities lived, there remain very few signs that they were even there. In many cases, thousands of people were destroyed without trace. But as you look around, there are still things to remind us that the Jews who lived there were real people, with real lives, whose memory must be preserved.

Still today, survivors of the Holocaust write, talk, and bear witness to the destruction of the European Jews.

Through their stories, the memory of those communities lives on and we learn about them. Soon, survivors will no longer be able to tell their stories. Then, the 800 children from Tarnow, along with almost six million other victims, will only have us to remember them. That is partly why learning about their experiences should be a reminder to us in the future.

Cutlery in the open air at the Kanada section of Auschwitz-Birkenau.

A candle in memory of the dead placed in one of the crematorium ovens at Auschwitz-Birkenau.

The tell-tale sign of a removed mezuzah, Zakatno Street, Tarnow.

Survivor Michael Lee wanders across the front of the memorial at Auschwitz-Birkenau at the end of the ramp where his family were selected to die.

Block 25: In the Women's Camp, women selected to die waited here for certain death.

Nathan and Jill pivnik: Bendzin, site of the former great synagogue.

Hide and seek: Child playing around the remnant of the bimah in the Alte Shul (Old Synagogue), Tarnow

memorials

As people try to understand what the Holocaust means for them today, all over the world, museums, memorials, and centres of education have been created.

YAD VASHEM Israel's national institution of Holocaust remembrance and education, Yad Vashem was founded in 1945 in memory of the lost Jewish Communities of Europe. 'Yad Vashem' means 'a monument and a name'. Since its creation, Yad Vashem has become a key centre of international scholarship and education about the Holocaust. It is visited not only by Israelis and tourists, but also by foreign leaders on state visits.

AUSCHWITZ MEMORIAL MUSEUM Today the site of the former concentration camp at Auschwitz has been preserved as a museum and memorial to the victims of the Nazis who were murdered there. There are several parts to the museum, but most importantly, the brick barracks that served as the Nazi headquarters now houses an historical exhibition. Close by is the huge site of Auschwitz-Birkenau, where the gas chambers were situated. Visitors can go here to see where these events took place, to learn the history and to reflect on it.

UNITED STATES HOLOCAUST MEMORIAL MUSEUM The national Holocaust Museum of the United States opened in 1993 after 13 years' work. The United States Holocaust Memorial Museum has a different emphasis to Yad Vashem, in that it seeks to address what this experience might mean for an American audience, who did not experience the Holocaust and whose primary memories - somewhat like those of people in our own country - are of liberation of the camps by their soldiers at the end of World War II.

THE HOLOCAUST CENTRE, BETH SHALOM Because it is in the UK, Beth Shalom is not a site of the Holocaust but a place of memorial and learning. The centre opened in 1995, and is unique as the initiative of a Christian family. It has gained an international reputation for its sensitivity and educational excellence.

hope for the *future*

These places exist in the hope that through memorials and through education, we can prevent anything like the Holocaust happening again. Genocides have taken place since 1945, and there will probably be more. However, the more aware people like you and me become about these issues, the greater the hope that just maybe, when we are in a position to help people in danger, we will recognise the warning signs and do something about them while we can.

CHRONOLOGY

1919 German Workers Party founded in Munich.

Adolf Hitler joins, 19 September.

1923 Antisemitic publication, Der Stürmer, first published.

The Munich Putsch led by Göring and Storm Troopers.

Hitler serves 9 months for his part in the Putsch.

1925 Nazi Party re-formed.

SS created as a 'protection' force.

1930 Nazis receive 18 per cent of the national vote.

1932 Nazis become single largest party in July election.

1933 Hitler appointed Chancellor.

Reichstag burned - Communists blamed.

'Enabling Act' transfers power to Hitler's Cabinet.

Dachau concentration camp set up.

Boycott of Jewish goods/businesses.

Public book burning.

1934 'Night of the Long Knives' - Leaders of the SA killed by Hitler's SS.

President von Hindenburg dies.

Hitler declares himself Führer of the Third Reich.

1935 Nuremberg laws - anti-Jewish racial laws - introduced.

1936 Olympic Games held in Berlin.

1938 Anschluss in Austria.

Evian Conference.

Kristallnacht.

1939 All Jews to be removed by emigration.

Germany invades Poland: Britain and France declare war.

Star of David badge becomes obligatory.

Jewish Councils set up.

1940 Ghettos sealed off.

1941 Operation Barbarossa begins.

Einsatzgruppen begin slaughtering Jews.

Heydrich receives orders to prepare for the 'Final Solution'.

Zyklon B tested at Auschwitz.

Babi Yar - 33,771 Jews shot in two days near Kiev.

German Jews 'relocated' to the 'East'.

Chelmno death camp becomes operational.

1942 Wannsee Conference, Berlin, makes the 'Final Solution' official.

Operation Reinhard begins - destruction of Polish Jewry.

Deportation of Dutch Jews begins.

Deportation of Jews from Warsaw.

1943 Warsaw ghetto uprising.

Danish people rescue most of the Danish Jews.

1944 Germans occupy Hungary; Adolf Eichmann is placed in charge of 'Jewish Matters'.

Request from Jewish leaders to Britain to bomb rail lines to Auschwitz.

Bomb plot against Hitler fails.

Auschwitz ceases to operate as a killing centre.

1945 Auschwitz liberated.

Bergen-Belsen liberated by British forces.

Hitler commits suicide in his Berlin bunker.

The Germans surrender to the Allies - May 7.

Survivors continue to die of malnutrition and disease. Somehow, they had to find the strength to build a new life.